THE LIFE & WORK

OF

LUKE FILDES, R.A.

By

DAVID CROAL THOMSON

London

J.S.Virtue & co., limited

1895.

FAIR QUIET AND SWEET REST. BY LUKE FILDES, R.A   (*. 77.)

LUKE FILDES, R.A.

TO write a lengthy monograph on an artist who is happily still in active work is a task which naturally has its limitations. It is not required from the writer to be too exact as to the artistic quality displayed in the works under consideration; nor that, in the current expression of the hour, it should be his endeavour to "place" the painter in the precise niche he is to occupy for all time coming. It is in fact almost impossible to do so, for an artist like Mr. Luke Fildes has capabilities and potentialities which may, even yet, lead him in directions widely differing from the work produced in the past.

My plan, therefore, lies more in the way of exposition of the aims of the painter, with the work he has recently produced, of which examples are exhibited throughout these pages; and how far his aims have been suitably developed in his productions.

In the past, the nearest painter-personality to Mr. Fildes has been Sir David Wilkie, an artist whose fame has seen a certain eclipse, but who is now, and probably definitely, relegated to a very important position amongst painters; and whose works collectors eagerly compete for in the auction-rooms.

Sir David Wilkie, it is now fully acknowledged, was greatest as a painter of the people of his own day—the peasants amongst whom he was brought up, and whose pleasures and sorrows he so thoroughly understood. 'The Penny Wed-ding,' 'Blind Man's Buff,' and many others, attest Wilkie's power of sympathy, while his so-called more ambitious pseudo-classic works leave the onlookers entirely cold.

An analogy may be found in the experience of Mr. Fildes. His first pictures were taken from the life by which he found

THE PLOUGHBOY. BY LUKE FILDES, R.A.   (*. 8.)

himself surrounded—'The Casual Ward,' his observations in London, 'The Penitent,' his experience in the country. Then, attracted, as every one must be who visits Venice, by the beautiful Italian girls with their charming costumes and exhilarating colour, he painted Venetian pictures for several years. No one has drawn them better, and they mark bright and pleasant epochs in the life of the artist.

Happily Mr. Fildes has not spent too long with the Venetians, and in 'The Doctor' we welcome him back to English ways and English subjects, with which all his warm sympathies lie. 'The Doctor,' of which I shall treat a little later, is a typical subject for the English-speaking people, and its extraordinary success in every part of the world shows that even to foreigners the idea appeals with singular force. Again, the portrait of the Princess of Wales aroused an enthusiasm that sent the *Graphic* Christmas number, where it first appeared, up to

. An Original Study for "The Casuals.'
(*p. iv.*)

larger figures than ever before, while Messrs. Agnew's beautiful etching of the same picture is one of the most popular plates of the day.

An artist's talent ought to be the crystallisation of the thought of his age, and no living painter, either British or foreign, has acquired and retained a wider popularity. He knows exactly what will touch his audience, and never was this

An Original Study for 'The Casuals.'
(*p. iv.*)

gift more strongly betrayed than in his drawing of the Empty Chair of Charles Dickens, a drawing, issued in the *Graphic*, and still to be seen in all parts of the country as one of the most treasured pictures.

The late Phillip Gilbert Hamerton was one of the first of the more serious critics to allow Mr. Fildes's claim to the greatest qualities, and his verdict in "Man in Art" is that "amongst English artists of the present day Mr. Fildes is one of those who have found their way most directly to the human heart."

In the eyes of many lovers of the Fine Arts the very fact

The Original Sketch for 'Applicants for Admission to a Casual Ward.' By Luke Fildes, R.A.
By Permission of the Proprietors of "The Graphic." (*p. iv.*)

that Mr. Fildes has touched the popular heart pronounces him a painter to be considered only on the level of the illustrator. But those who have seen his pictures, or, better still, have seen him at work, and carefully examined his technique or method of applying the colour to the canvas, know that his is not the slipshod, popular surface painting common enough in all directions. He sees through his brush to his audience, and he sympathises and understands them in the way a Burns or a Piers Plowman did, and the result of his labour is no less great.

As detailed in a later chapter, Mr. Fildes passed through some trying experiences ; but it was the untimely death of Charles Dickens, involving the stoppage of the mysterious unfinished " Edwin Drood " he was illustrating, that decided him to follow the course he now desired to follow.

Having, at this time, no one to think of but himself, he determined to risk everything, and become a painter in oils, and he set up his easel in the house in King Henry's Road in north-west London to which he had recently removed.

A SKETCH FOR 'THE CASUALS.'   (*p. iv.*)

He was sufficiently ambitious, and it was on a canvas nine feet long that he began as an oil painter to tempt fortune— never, however, fickle with him.

It had been through Sir John Millais' kindness and perception that young Fildes had been introduced to Charles Dickens, and now that Dickens was dead, and he had determined to leave small work, it was naturally to Millais that he went at this great crisis in his life.

This is not the place to make a panegyric on Sir John Everett Millais, but some day it will be known how kind and helpful this famous painter has been to his younger fellow-artists. His hearty and bluff way was directly suited to the young painter's temperament, and the youthful artist felt he could lay his project before the artist who had himself se-cured so much distinction.

The question for Millais to decide was with which of two small sketches submitted to him should he begin his career as a painter. One of these drawings Mr. Fildes had prepared for the publication, *Once a Week*, which required illustrations

to accompany poems. As a rule, the artist made his drawings, and the budding Lau-reate was thereby in-spired to write a son-net. This was 'Fair Quiet and Sweet Rest,' and the other compo-sition submitted to Mr. Millais, as he was then, was the sketch of 'Applicants for Admission to a Casual Ward.'

A SKETCH FOR 'THE CASUALS.'   (*p. iv.*)

Mr. Millais had no hesitation in saying that, to begin, it would be better to take the 'Fair Quiet and Sweet Rest' for one reason, and that naturally an important one—' The Casuals ' might not so easily find a market. There was worldly wisdom, as well as artistic pru-dence, in the advice. Undoubtedly the first was, commercially speaking, a far better picture for sale, but equally certainly (and this probably weighed chiefly with the experienced painter), ' The Casuals' was a far more difficult picture to paint, and the practice acquired in the production of the 'Fair Quiet and Sweet Rest' would make the way easier for the grander picture.

The 'Fair Quiet and Sweet Rest ' was hung on the line in the Royal Academy Exhibition of 1872, and in the centre of one of the walls. Like Turner, Mr. Fildes has ever been favoured by the Royal Academy, and equally with Turner is he devoted to its best interests. Other than Millais, young Fildes, at twenty-seven, did not know any of the Royal Academicians, and it is safe to say that if he had been on intimate terms with them he would not have availed himself of their friendship. In any case it is a fact that he knew only one, and yet his first picture was not only accepted but placed on the line, and in a posi-tion of honour on the walls.

The critics were a little disconcert-ed with the appear-ance of this work on the walls of the Royal, Academy, and it was stated

A STUDY FOR A CHILD FOR 'THE WIDOWER.' BUT NOT USED IN THE FINAL COMPOSITION. (*p. viii.*)

A STUDY FOR 'THE WIDOWER.'   *(p. viii.)*

A STUDY FOR THE WIDOWER.'   *(p. viii.)*

by one or two of them that the new painter was a distant imitator of Walker, Pinwell, Boughton (!), and Leslie (!), and *The Times* concluded a lengthy description of the picture by the remark :— "Mr. Fildes has made a gallant but not a great *début*. Do not let him allow his younger friends to persuade him that he has really done much more than given proof that he can handle brushes and colours deftly and effectively." A very fair verdict this, and one in which the artist would now probably be the first to acquiesce. The picture, of which an illustration is given on page 1, was sold at a good price in the artist's studio before going to the Academy to an astute picture dealer in the Haymarket.

The subject of the line-engraving published herein under the title of 'The Sweet River,' was originally named, somewhat sarcastically, 'Simpletons,' a title the artist may have meant to be as much suggestive of innocent flirtation as of love-making become ridiculous. It is to be observed also that it was painted the year before he married Miss Fanny Woods, the sister of his great friend, Mr. Henry Woods, now also a Royal Academician. In any case we have Mr.

reaches. Two lovers, having found a quiet nook where reeds and trees lend a friendly shadow, and water lilies deck the water, are holding happy communion together. The lady's left hand is not yet decorated with a ring, and the eventful question has not yet been asked and answered, but it is evident, even to the pug dog, that the psychological moment is not far off. The girl turns her head from her lover, and dips her dainty finger in the Sweet River which, in the future, will be to her the most beautiful of flowing waters.

It was not until 1874 that 'The Casuals' was exhibited, for the artist had been working in a leisurely way, feeling tolerably safe from the financial point of view, because of his instant success in the 1872 Academy.

From the illustrations it will be seen how greatly this picture differs from the 'Sweet Rest.' In sentiment and subject two ideas could scarcely be further apart. Yet both were the outcome of personal observation. The 'Sweet Rest' was, of course, an actual experience on the Thames; but the 'Casuals' was a vision granted to a great artist in a moment of inspiration. Going home late, the young artist—he was only twenty-nine when the picture was exhibited — was struck by the terrible pathos, as he himself has expressed it, of a sight he had seen one night when wandering in search of subjects :

"I had been to a dinner party, I think, and happened to return by a police-station, when I saw an awful crowd of poor wretches applying for permits to lodge in the Casual Ward. I made a note of the scene, and after that often went again, making friends with the policeman and talking with the people themselves. Then was my chance, and I at

THE ORIGINAL STUDY IN OILS FOR 'THE WIDOWER.' BY LUKE FILDES, R.A.   *(p. viii.)*   *(Copyright registered.)*

Fildes' approval for the present title, which is much more reminiscent of the artist's work than the other. 'The Sweet River' is of course the Thames, but it may be equally possible to find it on the Severn, the Tyne, or the Clyde, in their upper

once began to make studies for my *Graphic* picture. From that I elaborated the large canvas afterwards exhibited at the Academy."

This was, indeed, the work that first brought Mr. Fildes

APPLICANTS FOR ADMISSION TO A CASUAL WARD. By LUKE FILDES, R.A. (p. iv

By Permission of the Governors and Trustees of Holloway College, Egham.

into notice, and it is interesting to hear his stories of his visits and his chats with the poor casuals. The scene shows a lot of shivering wretches, of all sorts and conditions. "The leering, indifferent loafer, the bloated drunkard, the family who had just been sold up and forced to seek the cruel hospitality of the streets—father, mother, and children—involuntarily formed into a pathetic group; the policeman—not a Bumble, but a man not case-hardened into indifference to suffering—is instructing a man who has evidently seen better days how to obtain admission; the rain is pouring down, and swept by the wind into

A STUDY FOR THE ELDER GIRL IN ' THE WIDOWER.'
(p. viii.)

The painting is now in the Royal Holloway College at Egham, where it is one of the treasures of a notable collection, and it is to one of the last acts of the late Sir Geo. Martin Holloway that I am indebted, with the consent of the governors, to its appearance in these pages. The sketches give an idea of some of the studies necessary for the completion of such a work—the canvas is again nine feet long—but the most interesting is the first general sketch on our second page. This was the artist's original idea of the subject, and, by comparison with the reproduction of the large picture on page 5, it will be noted how faithful he has remained to his *première pensée*.

In 1874 Mr. Fildes first visited Venice, and a separate chapter tells of his achievements there.

In 1875 Mr. Fildes painted ' Betty '—a fresh and charming picture of a country milkmaid—of which we give an illustration at page 23. This was afterwards published in colour by the *Illustrated London News*, and is one of the

A STUDY FOR CHILDREN IN ' THE WIDOWER.'   (p. viii.)

the faces of the miserable crowd. The grim walls of the station form a background, whose gloom is suggested rather than shown by the flickering light of a dim lantern hung over

LUKE FILDES, R.A., PAINTING ' THE RETURN OF THE PENITENT.' BY HENRY WOODS, R.A.
FROM THE PAINTING IN THE COLLECTION OF HOLBROOK GASKELL, ESQ.   (p. viii.)

the station door." " In time," Mr. Fildes continued, " some of them got to know me, and I would tell them to come round to my house for a job, and I used to induce them to sit to me "

best known of the artist's works. Mr. Fildes had just returned from studying in Venice, but there is nothing about ' Betty ' that is not absolutely English. Two years after exhi-

THE RETURN OF THE PENITENT. BY LUKE FILDES, R.A. (Contd.)

FROM THE PICTURE IN THE COLLECTION OF HOLBROOK GASKELL, ESQ.

biting 'The Casuals' came the picture, equal in size and almost equal in importance, of 'The Widower.' On account of copyright property, the privilege of here giving a reproduction of this picture, which is now in the Art Gallery at Sydney, is withheld.

I have, however, the copyright owner's kind permission to publish reproductions of the original sketches made for the picture. The study in oil of the complete picture (page 4) is nearly the same as the finished work, the principal difference being that the widower—as in one of the small sketches—has the child on his right knee. The widower himself (page 4) is seen in two attitudes— one having the sick child on his left arm—the position chosen ultimately for the large picture —and the other with the child on the right arm. The eldest of the family, who takes charge during the father's enforced absence, is shown at page 6, looking down mournfully at her ill sister. On the same page is given the children, too young to understand the realities of life, who have been discussing their evening meal ; and, lastly, there is the child (not used in the final picture), eager and happy in the midst of doubt and grief.

'The Widower' appeared in the Royal Academy Exhibition of 1876, and it achieved a success at least equal

PHYLLIS. BY LUKE FILDES, R.A.   (*p. x.*)
FROM THE PICTURE IN THE ROYAL ACADEMY DIPLOMA GALLERY.
BY PERMISSION OF MESSRS. KNOEDLER & CO., NEW YORK,
THE PUBLISHERS OF THE LARGE PLATE.

the picture without emotion would not be a desirable person to know." The success of 'The Widower' was so great that many people expected Mr. Fildes would be chosen Associate of the Academy. but there were older men whose claims were considered superior, and it was not until three years later, 1879, that he entered the outer apartments of the Royal Academy. There is no doubt, however, that 'The Widower' secured him his election, for he showed nothing in 1878.

It was not until 1879 that he exhibited the 'Return of the Penitent,' of which, by permission of Holbrook Gaskell, Esq., a reproduction is given on page 7, the first that has been made of the picture. Another aspect of the picture is seen in the painting by Mr. Henry Woods, R.A., brother-in-law to Mr. Fildes, also in Mr. Holbrook Gaskell's collection, which was exhibited under the title of 'A Country Studio.' This is a representation of Mr. Fildes in the act of painting studies for 'The Return of the Penitent,' the large picture itself being seen in the barn wherein it really was painted. Through the doorway Mr. Fildes is visible, painting from a country lass a study to be afterwards incorporated with the large work.

The subject of 'The Return of the Penitent' is only fairly well expressed in the title. The

to 'The Casuals.' The critics were again a little puzzled how to take this picture. *The Times*, while admitting its force, scolded the artist for his representation of intense painfulness and overstrained expression. "The painter is under a mistake," said the Thunderer, "who brings big dirty boots, squalling and scrambling children, parental and sisterly love . . . into such close contact." The *Morning Post* more readily understood the artist's position, and judiciously praised him for his "simple truth and homely eloquence," which were altogether irresistible. The notice went with full detail into the *minutiæ* of the scene, and concluded with the remarkable words : — "The man who could view

artist had thought of calling it 'The Prodigal,' and only at the last moment was persuaded, half against his will, to give the subject its present name. Into the pleasant street of a prosperous English village the Penitent has wandered back to her birthplace, heartbroken and weary with her bitter experience of human life. But, as the lines from Byron said under the title in the Academy catalogue,

> " Every woe a tear may claim,
> Except an erring woman's shame,"

and the neighbours view her presence with but cold-hearted charity. Men may pardon such sin, but women either dare not or cannot : dare not, most probably. because even to seem to countenance a straying from the path of virtue would destroy the foundation of the family and of society, and the true womanly instinct is happily against such wanderings.

JESSICA. BY LUKE FILDES, R.A. (*p. x.*)
FROM THE SHAKESPEARE'S HEROINES SERIES.
WITH THE CONSENT OF MESSRS. SAMPSON LOW, MARSTON & CO.

The Penitent has come to find her former home dismantled, and her parents dead. Long time has she been dallying in the haunts of erring pleasure, and in the interval the father and mother who so proudly looked on their beautiful daughter have sunk their gray hairs with sorrow in the grave because of their offspring's fall.

All this is known to those who lived at hand, and now at the sight of the too-well-remembered figure, they group themselves together, pursing their lips in the just disdain of moral motherhood. A man checks his horse as he recognises the Penitent, and he is the first to give her a kindly thought. It is his own girl beside him who has drawn his attention to the crouching figure, and his heart does not harden like the womenfolk's, and he will gladly help her if he can.

The English village where the scene is laid is typical, and it is to be observed that the artist seeks to gain nothing dramatically from the surrounding objects. In place of being sad, the village is cheerful, and even gay; the sky is bright; and the whole scene suggests happiness rather than despair. Such points of hope add to the picture, and leave the spectator in no doubt that, although weeping may endure for a night, hope—if not joy—will arise in the morning.

This picture, again, received great attention in the Academy, and the critics now showed themselves well disposed to the young painter. This was before the day when it has been discovered that subject in a picture makes it too interesting,

in a literary sense, to be artistic, and there were few who felt called on to say anything but praise. *The Standard* spoke of the impressiveness of the picture, "impressive, not because of its subject, so easily sensational, but because of the fitting union of high qualities of inventor, observer, and craftsman which the canvas displays."

The election of Mr. Fildes to the Associateship of the Royal Academy, in 1879, had the unconscious effect of making him very difficult to please with his work. This is an experience not at all uncommon, and many artists have been affected in the same way. In 1880 Mr. Fildes did not exhibit in London, and in 1881 he sent only three unimportant canvases, the results of recent visits to Venice; and in 1882 he exhibited only another small picture.

Meanwhile he had been preparing a very large work, and to the Royal Academy Exhibition of 1883 he sent 'The Village Wedding,' of which, by the courtesy of Messrs. Agnew & Sons, a reproduction is given on page 11. For years some of Mr. Fildes's admirers had found his pathetic vein so strong as to be a little non-attractive, and he determined to please every one by painting the event which ought to be the happiest in the life of both man and woman. Here, indeed, was a change of subject, and the picture proved that the artist's admirers were not far wrong—that he could paint happiness as well as misery, and that the creator of 'The Casuals' and 'The Return of the Penitent' was not always in a pensive frame of mind.

A CHILD OF VENICE. BY LUKE FILDES, R.A. (*p. x.*)

Many are the stories which the painter tells of his experiences when painting this picture. The bridegroom was, unwittingly, the same model he had painted on the horse in

D

'The Penitent' several years before. Seeking for a model, he went to a farmer friend in Berkshire to tell him his difficulty. The farmer thought he knew a suitable man—a shepherd recently married—and they walked over the fields to see him. Long before they reached the shepherd, the countryman had recognised the artist, yet he kept his peace. The bargain was struck and the bridegroom secured, but the painter had a haunting notion of having seen the man before, and, while painting him, he at last asked him the question. "Oh, yes, sir," he said, "you painted me on a horse years ago at South Stoke-on-Thames, and I knew you the moment you entered the field with my master."

The stalwart guardsman with the mother of the bride on one arm, staid but satisfied, and with the frolicsome younger sister on the other, gave the artist some trouble, for the model from the Guards' barracks was nervous at the presence of ladies, and blushed very uncomfortably when he was asked to give his arms to other models stationed alongside.

It required a great deal of artistic courage to paint this picture; a bride is always interesting, but a bridegroom is fair game, and to paint a man in a tall hat, carrying a lady's parasol, who was, moreover, a bridegroom, without making him ridiculous, was no small achievement. In other ways the artist encountered unexpected difficulties : the girls to the right, one throwing a slipper, were at first designed to be on a balcony of a house, but their presence so high up outbalanced the picture, and they were ultimately brought to stand in the side-walk, greatly to the advantage of the composition.

Although the popularity of this picture never was so great as 'The Casuals' or 'The Doctor,' 'The Village Wedding' is undoubtedly one of the truest of Mr. Fildes' representations of English life. It has found its way to all parts of the world, and many a Colonist can trace likenesses to friends in the Old Land amongst those assembled so picturesquely in 'The Village Wedding.'

We have now reached the time when Mr. Fildes devoted himself for several years almost entirely to painting Venetian pictures, and these are treated in a special chapter to themselves. In 1887 he made his first attempt at portrait painting, as a separate art from subject painting, and to the Royal Academy Exhibition for that year he sent the portrait of Mrs. Fildes ; and this was the first of the series of queenly portraits he has been painting since then.

A CHALK STUDY. BY LUKE FILDES, R.A.

Portraits being also dealt with separately, we shall pass on to 1880, when Mr. Fildes exhibited one of the most attractive of all his beautiful single figures. This picture, called 'A Schoolgirl' in the Academy catalogue, has been published under the title 'Phyllis,' by the eminent American house, Messrs. Knoedler & Co., of New York, who have kindly allowed the reproduction to adorn these pages. The title 'A Schoolgirl' is retained in the Diploma Gallery of the Royal Academy, where the picture has been deposited. Each Royal Academician on his election is required to give a specimen of his art worth at least £100 to the permanent gallery of the Academy. This collection, it may be observed, is housed in Burlington House above the offices of the Academy, and is open free every day, and its contents are interesting and valuable. Seldom if ever does a Royal Academician give a work about which there could be any discussion as to its being worth a hundred pounds, and it may safely be said that several times that sum would not purchase such a beautiful work as this.

'Phyllis,' on her way to school, slate under her arm, and satchel over it, scans her lesson-book with a calmness that does honour to her erudition. It is a warm day, and her dress is thrown open and her hat tossed on her pretty head without much concern for outward appearances, but her *négligée* style becomes her well, and in any case she makes a pretty picture.

Another of the illustrations, 'Jessica,' was painted about the same time for the series of pictures called 'Shakespeare's Heroines.' This was one of Mr. W. L. Thomas's successful *Graphic* schemes, whereby all the famous heroines of the immortal bard were idealised by living English painters. The subject allotted to Mr Fildes was 'Jessica,' the charming daughter of Shylock the Jew, beloved of Lorenzo, the friend of the Merchant of Venice.

> "Alack, what heinous sin is it in me
> To be ashamed to be my father's child !
> But though I am a daughter to his blood,
> I am not to his manners. O Lorenzo,
> If thou keep promise, I shall end the strife—
> Become a Christian, and thy loving wife."

The other illustrations include 'The Ploughboy' (page 1), painted in 1875, a little study in oil, which renders a purely English subject with all the painter's skill; and also 'Marianne,' a Venetian child's head, which has not yet left the artist's studio. The colour of the latter is low in tone but perfect in harmony, and in fine quality of free and masterly brushwork

THE VILLAGE WEDDING. By LUKE FILDES, R.A. (A.ix.)

By Permission of Messrs. Agnew & Sons, the Publishers of the Large Plate.

There only remains 'The Doctor' to discuss, and we have arrived at the present time in Mr. Fildes' work. What he may attempt in the future is not easy to foretell, but it appears probable that he will never return to Venetian pictures, and it is also likely that he will cease to devote so much of his art to portrait painting. Yet it would not be safe to say he will paint subject pictures connected with English peasant life only, in years to come. As an artist Mr. Fildes cannot but know that his greatest successes have been with his peasant pictures, successes which are likely to be permanent because of their appeal to a healthy sentiment universal in human nature. Requests of the collectors and connoisseurs also cannot be neglected, and it is therefore more than probable, and it is with gladness I come to the conclusion, that Mr. Fildes' work in the future will consist of subject pictures connected with the inhabitants of the British Isles.

The picture of 'The Doctor' was a long time in preparation, and for several months the great studio in Melbury Road was witness to the painter's project. After many studies Mr. Fildes had the interior of a cottage erected inside his own studio. This was carefully planned and properly built with rafters and walls and window, all as afterwards expressed in the finished picture. One side of the studio was occupied with this cottage, and it was from thence that the light and shade of the picture was composed. Well do I remember the first time Mr. Fildes mentioned this picture to me. This was long before the cottage was built inside the studio and before more than the first idea had shaped itself in the artist's mind. "Do you remember 'The Casuals,'" said Mr. Fildes, "and 'The Widower,' and 'The Return of the Penitent'? Well, to me, the new subject will be more pathetic than any, more terrible perhaps, but yet more beautiful."

Such a suggestion roused my curiosity, but it was not until after the picture had been finished I understood all the artist's meaning.

The drawing below, by Mr. Reginald Cleaver, gives a fair idea of the artist's methods of study for this picture. The large canvas on the easel is painted on without a mahl-stick to rest the hand. In the background is seen the half-cottage the artist built to assist him in the realisation of the surroundings and of the play of light and shade on the figures.

Mr. Fildes made very few studies for this picture, although he sketched many cottages, both English and Scottish, before he decided the interior. In north-east Scotland—in Moray—he made drawings from various peasant dwellings, but the room painted he never saw in actual completeness.

The sketch we reproduce is the only real study made for 'The Doctor,' and it will be observed with some curiosity that, as in 'The Widower,' the artist has ultimately decided to turn his principal figure round. In the last-named picture the widower is altered from the first study, and again in 'The

overcome with terrible dread, stand in the background trusting their doctor even while their hearts fail.

At the cottage window the dawn begins to steal in—the

THE ORIGINAL SKETCH IN OIL FOR 'THE DOCTOR.' BY LUKE FILDES, R.A. (*p. xii.*)

Doctor,' as may be seen by comparing the illustration here presented and the etching by Mr. Salles, that the Doctor is reversed. This sketch has not hitherto been reproduced. The various minute changes, not, however, quite clearly rendered in the preliminary sketch study, are very interesting to trace and compare with the large picture.

This composition of 'The Doctor' has been recognised by the medical profession as a great and lasting compliment to the whole body. No more noble figure than the doctor could be imagined—the grave anxiety, supported by calm assurance in his own knowledge and skill, not put forward in any self-sufficient way, but with dignity and patience, following out the course his experience tells him is correct; the implicit faith of the parents, who, although deeply moved and almost

dawn that is the critical time of all deadly illnesses—and with it the parents again take hope into their hearts, the mother hiding her face to escape giving vent to her emotion, the father laying his hand on the shoulder of his wife in encouragement of the first glimmerings of the joy which is to follow.

The picture of 'The Doctor' has been promised to the nation by Mr. Henry Tate. It has been published in large size by Messrs. Thomas Agnew & Sons, by whose courtesy we have been allowed to prepare the etching frontispiece to this monograph. In Mr. Tate's Westminster Gallery, when it is opened next year, the painting itself will be free to all the world to visit and discuss. The etching we publish has been a labour of love to Mr. Salles, and his refined interpretation of the picture has received the artist's complete approval.

LUKE FILDES, R.A.,

AS A PAINTER OF VENETIANS.

SKETCH FOR THE
VENETIAN FRUIT-SELLER.
(p. xviii.)

WHEN Mr. Fildes went to Venice in 1874, the first truth that came home to him was the perfect naturalness of the Venetian people. No one attempted, or seemed even remotely to wish, to occupy another sphere but the one they were born into. The fruit-seller did not aim at being a merchant, the gondolier did not seek to be an officer, the flower-girls did not ape being ladies of fashion. Each was perfectly content to fulfil the work allotted to them, and they dressed accordingly.

Mr. Fildes' experience of models in England had been often a constant source of worry, until he had come to the belief that the peasant of England was a thing of the past. Jean François Millet and Bastien Lepage, in France, had witnessed the last of the true peasantry of Western Europe, and it even appeared to him doubtful if Bastien's peasants were genuine people of the soil, and not made-up models found in perfection only in the studio dressing-room. No more was a contented peasantry to be found in the country districts of England; the smock-frock was never worn in reality, but donned occasionally as a curiosity and only by old people almost dying out. The school board had taught the people to be clerks when they would have been more happy to have been ploughmen, and the black coat for Sunday and the tall silk hat were considered the goals of every working man's life.

All over the world, however, this change has been in operation, with or without schools and board managers. In Holland the ridiculous would-be gentility of the peasants has often culminated in a bonnet of Paris fashion cocked jauntily over the wonderful headgear of white cap and silver ornaments. In France the blouse is still retained in many parts, and it may be that there is a truer French peasantry than elsewhere. In Scotland, of course, the kilt is chiefly worn by noblemen's retainers, who find it their interest to be picturesque. While in Ireland a man does not properly hold up his head until he has a chimney-pot hat to heighten the esteem of himself and his neighbours.

NINA: A VENETIAN STUDY. BY LUKE FILDES, R.A. (p. xvi.)

AN ITALIAN FLOWER-GIRL. BY LUKE FILDES, R.A. (*p. xvi.*)
BY PERMISSION OF MESSRS. BOUSSOD, VALADON & CO., THE PUBLISHERS OF THE LARGE PLATE.

All these difficulties of class dress seemed to vanish in Venice, and there Mr. Fildes found ready to his hand scores of models, in a perfect blaze of colour, of the most attractive order. All he had to do was to go out to the market-place and entice a model to pose for him in her every-day dress, on conditions neither difficult for the painter nor irksome to the sitter.

In 1880 Pettenkofen exercised a strong influence on all painters in Venice, and, to a certain extent, Mr. Fildes owned his sway. This influence scarcely showed itself in his work, for Pettenkofen paints mostly small pictures, while Fildes, in nearly all his Venetian work, indulged in large canvases.

understand the anxious hearts amongst the gondoliers to secure a smile of recognition from the Venetian beauty.

The painting of the flowers in this picture is one of the best things Mr. Fildes has done in still life, while the vivacity of the colouring makes the picture one well suited to lighten the houses of dull London. The 'Italian Flower-Girl' hangs in a well-known corner house in Grosvenor Square, while the 'Venetian Flower-Girl' is the property of the City of Hamburg, having been included in Mr. Schwabe's gift to his native city.

In a flower-shop, near the Rialto, there is at the present time an attendant who has all the grace and beauty of Mr.

A FAIR VENETIAN. BY LUKE FILDES, R.A. (*p. xvi.*)

A DARK VENETIAN. BY LUKE FILDES, R.A. (*p. xvi.*)

The chief merit of Pettenkofen's method was the impasto he produced on the lighter parts of his composition, and the fine quality of objects in daylight shadow. But in this particular direction Mr. Fildes had very little to learn, for notwithstanding that he practically never had lessons in painting with oils, his quality of brushwork, even before he went to Venice, was vigorous and masterly.

One of the full-page illustrations renders the picture known under the title of 'An Italian Flower-Girl.' It is the same size and proportion as a somewhat similar picture, 'A Venetian Flower-Girl,' of which an outline by the artist is printed on page 17. From the reproduction it will be seen that Mr. Fildes was careful to choose a fair specimen of the race of flower-sellers. Well set-up, good-looking, and easy-natured, the girl is certain of admirers, and one can well

Fildes' picture; a girl, however, who knows too well her picturesque figure, and who is almost always to be seen outside her shop posing in an elegant attitude for passers-by to admire.

Amongst the other illustrations are examples of all the varieties of work accomplished by Mr. Fildes in Venice. As a head-piece we have one of the few views of the city he essayed to depict—the Dogana di Mare, almost opposite the steps leading to St. Mark's, and one of the landmarks of the beautiful sea city. 'Nina,' on the same page, is a study from life, of which only the head has been completed. 'The Fair Venetian,' 'The Dark Venetian,' following, are similar studies from life. 'The Balcony' is the first idea of a large picture never carried further; while the Heads drawn in crayons are examples of a different method of work.

AN AL FRESCO TOILETTE

FROM THE PAINTING BY LUKE FILDES, RA

BY PERMISSION OF MESSRS. BOUSSOD, VALADON & CO., PUBLISHERS OF THE LARGE PLATE

of a summer evening—after a very warm day—some young Venetian girls have been dressing each other's hair, while they and their neighbours gossip on passing events. The scene was witnessed by the artist and was mostly painted on the spot.

The background, it will be observed, is carefully designed and painted, and this lends character to the composition. The colour is

PENCIL SKETCH FOR 'AN AL-FRESCO TOILETTE.' (*p. xvii.*)

A VENETIAN GIRL. (*p. xvi.*)
A CHALK STUDY BY LUKE FILDES, R.A.

rich and firm, and the figures being well placed and at full length in the centre of the canvas, help to make the picture successful and satisfying. This work is now in the collection of Mr. George MacCulloch, whose pictures are to be illustrated and described in THE ART JOURNAL for 1896. The little preliminary sketch of the principal figure is freely put in and gives some idea of the artist's method of work.

The 'Venetian Fruit-Seller' was one of the earliest of Mr. Fildes' pictures painted in Venice, and it appeared as a plate in THE ART JOURNAL in 1881. As a result of his first visit, it shows how tentatively he went to work, contenting himself at first with the most ordinary incident of the day, similar to the morning call of the itinerant greengrocer to our kitchen

One of the most successful of his Italian pictures, 'An Al-Fresco Toilette,' of which we give a plate reproduction, was hung in the Royal Academy's Exhibition in 1889. This canvas gives the high-water mark of the Italian series, and it must be acknowledged that it is a very beautiful picture. In the cool

A VENETIAN FRUIT-SELLER. BY LUKE-FILDES, R.A., 1876. (*p. xvii.*)

F

THE BALCONY.
A SKETCH BY LUKE FILDES, R.A.   (*p. xvi.*)

has not revisited the Adriatic. It is, of course, impossible to foretell the future, and although in Art it is seldom the unexpected that happens, it is possible our artist may return some day to his love of Venetian life. But if it were necessary to forecast, I should certainly express my belief that never again will Venice claim Mr. Fildes as a worshipper. It may be, and in fact very likely will occur, that he will employ his many valuable studies of the people of Venice to produce other pictures, but it seems almost certain that, the phase once being past, he never will go back as a painter. Although it is absolutely the case that our artist was sincere in his Venetian pictures, painting only the side of Venetian life he could readily get to know, and with rare moderation not posing as one with special knowledge of their life and customs, the success of 'The Doctor' in the Academy of 1891 was too pronounced for Mr. Fildes to misinterpret the opinion of his contemporaries. Here, said the popular voice, is a painter who understands us and interprets our feelings, our sorrows and joys, our trials and temptations. But Venetians are little to us, the bulk of the British people; let him paint his own day and his own generation, and he will paint for all time as well as for the present.

Such, it may be, is the crystallisation of the thoughts of Mr. Fildes' best friends, and whilst his admirers gladly pay their tribute of admiration for the brilliant colouring and pretty forms of Venetian beauties, I, too, venture to hope he will in the future devote his powers to the realisation of the people whose feelings he can interpret as no other present-day painter can.

door. In the initial to this chapter a minute reproduction is given of one of Mr. Fildes' studies for this picture.

In 1885 'Venetians' was exhibited in the Royal Academy, and it was afterwards etched for THE ART JOURNAL, in 1887. This picture competes with 'An Al-fresco Toilette' for the chief place in the Venetian series, but the latter work, not painted for four years afterwards, has an approach to the artist's most natural style, which gives it one accomplishment the earlier picture a little lacks. The tail-piece below renders one of the studies Mr. Fildes made for 'Venetians,' a masterly treatment of landing steps in Venice, from which he painted the lower part of his large picture.

Since the 'Al-fresco Toilette' Mr. Fildes has painted only one or two Venetian subjects, and since that time he

A STUDY IN OIL OF STEPS IN VENICE. BY LUKE FILDES, R.A.   (*p. xviii.*)

LUKE FILDES, R.A.,

AS A PORTRAIT PAINTER.

IT will be readily admitted that it was an eminently natural proceeding for Mr. Fildes to become a painter of portraits, and the wonder is not that he has become one, but rather that he did not paint portraits from the beginning.

Yet it was only in 1887, when he had reached the fulness of his powers, and was a Royal Academician elect, that he painted a portrait, and his wife was the first subject. This picture, of which we have here a reproduction, was exhibited in the Royal Academy Exhibition of 1887, together with the portrait of Mrs. W. Lockett Agnew, and it is scarcely necessary to say these canvases attracted a great deal of attention. They gave the idea to many beautiful women to have their own portraits painted by one so facile, yet so faithful, with his brush.

It was two years later, however, before further portraits were exhibited, and in the exhibition at Burlington House, in 1889, appeared 'Sisters,' being portraits of two young ladies —the Misses Renton—one seated and the other standing, and as completely successful in tone and quality of colour as anything the artist has produced. Of this and of Mrs. James Bibby, painted in 1892, we give small illustrations, too small almost to do justice to their artistic quality, but space has forbidden larger reproductions.

Commissions now came in for portraits almost faster than the painter

MRS. FILDES. PAINTED BY LUKE FILDES, R.A.

wished, and at this time, and during the succeeding years, he has had more commissions than he could possibly satisfy, even although he did nothing to encourage them, but, persistently, rather the reverse. The Academy of 1890 contained, besides a portrait of a lady, a portrait of Mrs. Robert Borwick and of Mrs. Thomas Agnew, and the Academy of 1891, the same exhibition that contained 'The Doctor,' a portrait of Mrs. Lockett Agnew, another smaller work of brilliant success.

To the Exhibition of 1892 Mr. Fildes sent no less than five portraits, four of them of ladies— Mrs. Edwin Tate, daughter-in-law of the owner of 'The Doctor'; Miss Ethel Ismay, Mrs. Herbert S. Leon, and Mrs. Bibby. These were not all equally successful, and it is possible that the Nemesis of all portrait painters —that is, hasty production—was at work, and the artist wisely cur-

Mrs. James Bibby. By Luke Fildes, R.A.

The Sisters. By Luke Fildes, R.A.

tailed his labours for the following year.

In 1893 a further development took place, and Mr. Fildes exhibited his first man's portrait — Mr. G. B. Wieland, a presentation picture to the retiring secretary of the North British Railway. This portrait, although eminently characteristic of the sitter in its pose, and greatly admired by his friends, was perhaps less vigorous than might have been expected from the painter of 'The Doctor,' but this quality the artist has found in his still later portraits, and notably in the spirited likeness of Mr. Frank Bibby in the Royal Academy of 1895.

The 1893 exhibition also contained the 'Portrait of a Lady,' which, I think, is the most successful picture of a lady Mr. Fildes has painted. The charm of the expression, so English and yet so universal, marks this portrait as one of the most interesting of this end of the century, and there is no reason why in the future it should not be worth as much hard cash as the Lady Mulgrave by Gainsborough sold by auction in 1895 for £10,500. In many ways, in fact, these portraits resemble each other (a small reproduction of Lady Mulgrave is given at page 255 of THE ART JOURNAL for 1895), and if the work of the living artist has not yet that indefinable charm age only can render, otherwise the comparison is fair and not much to his disadvantage.

Since painting 'The Doctor' Mr. Fildes has not produced any subject picture, although gathering his strength and materials for a further great effort in the same direction. To the Exhibition of 1894 two ladies' portraits—in addition to that of the Princess of Wales —were sent by Mr. Fildes. In 1895 the position was varied a little by there being besides other two portraits of ladies, two portraits of men—Mr. Robert Yerburgh, M.P., and Mr. Frank Bibby, both the latter bold and vigorous.

It was in 1893 that Mr. Fildes was commissioned by the proprietors of the *Graphic* to paint the portraits of the Duke and Duchess of York, whose engagement had just been announced. The Prince and Princess were naturally very much engaged with all the preliminaries of their marriage, and as the time was comparatively short, Mr. Fildes went to the White Lodge for the sittings from Princess May, and to Marlborough House for those from Prince George.

The portraits— of which reproductions are here given by special permission from the Prince—gave the greatest satisfaction to the Royal Household. It was the first time for years that an English artist had been permitted to paint single portraits of royalty, and Mr. Fildes determined to make the most of the opportunity. The portraits were issued as coloured supplements, and

Portrait of a Lady. By Luke Fildes, R.A.

afterwards the originals were presented to the Duke and Duchess by the proprietors of the *Graphic*—a princely gift, and as such well appreciated by the Prince and Princess.

It was during the sittings of Prince George at Marlborough House that the idea of a portrait of the Princess of Wales was broached. Her Royal Highness came into the painting-room now and then—as did all the Household—to view the progress of the portraits, and she became so interested in the painter and his work that she expressed a willingness to sit to him, and this was eagerly supported by the Royal Family. For some years, they had wished the Princess to again have her portrait painted, and this opportunity gave them great pleasure, the portrait being presented to the Duke of York as a wedding gift.

This portrait of the Princess of Wales was also begun and

H.R.H. THE PRINCESS OF WALES. BY LUKE FILDES, R.A.
BY PERMISSION OF MESSRS. AGNEW, THE PUBLISHERS OF THE LARGE PLATE.

nearly completed at Marlborough House, and during the time Her Royal Highness became still more interested in

submitting it to the sitter, and the Princess felt a natural pleasure in observing the progress of this picture.

Mr. Fildes' method of allowing the sitter to witness the painting of the portrait may have some disadvantages, but these are outweighed by the interest taken by the sitter in the work, and therein entering into a kind of compact to make the result as satisfactory as possible.

It may not be inappropriate to mention here that one of the latest pictures Mr. Fildes has painted is a posthumous portrait of H.R.H. the late Duke of Clarence, for the Duke of York, as a wedding gift from the officers of the 10th Hussars, the regiment to which the late Duke belonged.

The Princess granted permission to the *Graphic* to reproduce her portrait in colours, and this was published in the Christmas number of that periodical in 1893, having therein a success quite extraordinary. Since then M. Lagillermie has made an etching of the portrait, and this has been quite

H.R.H. THE DUKE OF YORK. BY LUKE FILDES, R.A.

H.R.H. THE DUCHESS OF YORK. BY LUKE FILDES, R.A.

Mr. Fildes' method of work. It appears that, when having her portrait painted before this occasion, the artists invariably waited until their work was practically finished before

recently published by Messrs. Thomas Agnew & Sons, London and Manchester, who have given their consent to the little reproduction presented above.

EARLY SKETCH OF A CORNFIELD. A STUDY FOR THE BACKGROUND OF "BETTY." BY LUKE FILDES, R.A. (*p. vi*)

LUKE FILDES, R.A.

EARLY EXPERIENCES.

ALTHOUGH it would be far from correct to say that Mr. Fildes was born with a silver spoon in his mouth, yet it is an undoubted fact that he has never known what it is to be without the wherewithal to furnish the ordinary bread-and-butter of daily life. His forebears were of the middle-class stock which holds obedience to authority amongst its primary duties. As descendants of the Puritans they were strongly on the side of the Whigs and even of the Chartists, but notwithstanding their strong predilections for Radicalism, they were yet *bien bodies*, as the Scots say, a people with a certain property which they could hand on to their younger generations.

Born in Liverpool on October 18th, 1844, Mr. Fildes knew little or nothing of that busy sea-port. His father died while he was still young, and his mother marrying again, the boy was sent, when he was about eleven years old, to his father's mother, at Chester. Like Jean François Millet, therefore, Luke Fildes was brought up by his grandmother, and it is pleasant to know that the old lady lived until the painter achieved great success, even

THE STILE.
AN EARLY PICTURE BY LUKE FILDES, R.A.

although, as was the fact, she never realised how much her dearly loved grandson achieved by his own personality in the world of Art. The grandmother undertook the charge of the boy, but, as events turned out, the positions became more and more altered as the time went on, until, within a dozen years, they were actually reversed.

THE ARTIST IN 1866.

There does not appear to be any reason why the artistic instinct should have developed in our artist. So far as is known, none of his ancestors were inclined that way; they were, in fact, almost too serious people to think of Art as a profession, and it is quite possible that some ancient "Fyldes," as his family was called, experienced the first tendency of an artistic inclination, but suppressed, with a strong will, what he thought could only be the promptings of a tempter. Be this as it may, none of the family were artists; and, in any case, of their artistic aspirations no record exists.

Luke, as he was always called, was nevertheless continually making drawings. At every opportunity the pencil was in his hand, and by the time his boyhood had passed, he had decided to be an illustrator.

This was the highest ambition of his early youth. Of painters he practically knew nothing, and had not yet had any chance of learning of them. If he did know anything of their ways it was only to think of them as men specially gifted by the gods, and he did not even dream of entering their ranks. But an illustrator seemed possible—years it would take, he believed, and many hard knocks would be his in the pursuit, yet still it was possible—and towards that end he practically laid out his schemes, as soon as the power of drawing was expressed within him.

After a fair education at a good school in Chester — a boarding school, where he was a day pupil—he heard of the Science and Art classes in that city. Noticing a large bill announcing the hours of the school, young Fildes, at little more than thirteen years of age, and on absolutely his own initiative, determined to join the evening classes.

There he had the usual experience, uninteresting and unhappy freehand drawing, and all its wearisome details. The master was one who had no artistic sympathies, and feeling much the lack of encouragement and instruction, the youth sought it in other directions, and took lessons from a water-colour artist and teacher of drawing in Chester, of the name of Alfred Sumner. Mr. Fildes looks back with pleasure to his acquaintance with him, for in time this became less formal than is usual between master and pupil. Sumner — who has been many years in his grave now—had the artistic nature, and many long walks did he take with his pupil, descanting by the way on the Art dear to both. Walking through the country lanes, as Thomas Bewick did with his father, young Fildes imbibed a love of nature which has continued to grow ever since.

Becoming again unsettled in his mind and not yet certain that he was on the way to accomplish something worthy of living, he made inquiries as to other possibilities, and he heard of the reputation of the Art School at Warrington, and of the excellent teaching there, a place only twenty miles from Chester, but to the boy like another country. Telling his

"HETTY." FROM THE PAINTING BY LUKE FILDES, R.A.
WITH THE CONSENT OF A. M. MARSDEN, ESQ. (*p. vi.*)

grandmother his ambitions, the old lady made no difficulties but consented to let the boy go, and promised him support as long as he required it.

It was in 1861 that Luke Fildes joined the class at Warrington, that is, when he was sixteen. In the following year he travelled to London to see the Great Exhibition of 1862, and this was his first introduction to the possibilities of an artistic career.

In the short week he spent in the metropolis, he gave many hours to the galleries of pictures. There he saw the works of the men of whom he had only heard as in a dream. He began to realise that these men were once young like himself, that they, too, had their doubts and difficulties, over which they had triumphed by genius combined with industry. Industrious labour he already knew was within his power to accomplish, genius was still in the future. Possibly he heard of Turner's famous dictum, "I know no genius but the genius of hard work." In any case, he determined, while being ready to content himself with the position of an illustrator, to keep in his secret heart his wish to be a painter.

Confiding to the Warrington teacher his determination to return to London and seek the honours of his country at their fountain-head, the teacher advised him to try for a Scholarship in connection with the Art Schools at South Kensington. In October, 1863, he secured this prize of £50, and it encouraged him to still further effort, while it brought his ideal perceptibly nearer, for it took him to London to fulfil the terms of the study laid down for the prize-takers. The following year he again secured that sum of money, which lasted to the end of 1865. The authorities at South Kensington desired him to continue his studies, but he had now tasted the sweets of the more purely independent life of an artist, and he had strength of will enough to refuse.

In fact, young Fildes was now in relation with Mr. W. L. Thomas, since so deservedly celebrated as the founder of the *Graphic*. In 1865 the would-be illustrator began to make drawings on blocks, which Mr. Thomas, as the chief of one of the best wood-engraving establishments in London, had engraved for the various illustrated publications of the day. For a paper called *London Society*, in 1865, young Fildes prepared his maiden effort, and there were also blocks for the *Illustrated London News, Once a Week,* and others.

In 1866 Fildes again made a movement, and he applied to the Royal Academy to be admitted to their schools. As all the world knows, these schools are kept open free for the properly qualified student, and the examination is necessarily difficult. In order to gain the coveted distinction, our young artist put forth all his powers, and

WATER-COLOUR SKETCH, 'THE LOCKKEEPER'S COTTAGE.' BY LUKE FILDES, R.A.

he easily won his stool and easel in Burlington House.

As I have said, like Turner Mr. Fildes has been well treated by the Royal Academy from the first. In 1866 he was admitted student in the schools; in 1872 his first painting in oil, 'Fair Quiet and Sweet Rest,' was hung on the line. In 1874 his 'Applicants for Admission to a Casual Ward' had to be protected by a railing and policemen, in 1879 he was chosen Associate, and in 1887 a Royal Academician. Before his complete life can be written it is probable that still further honours will have to be added to this list.

"FOUND DEAD ON THE EMBANKMENT." STUDIES FOR AN ILLUSTRATION OF A STORY IN CHRISTMAS NUMBER OF "THE WORLD," 1878. (*p. xxviii.*)

PAINTED BY LUKE FILDES RA

THE ART JOURNAL

ENGRAVED BY C COUSEN

THE SWEET RIVER

OLD PUTNEY BRIDGE AND FULHAM CHURCH. PENCIL SKETCH FROM NATURE BY LUKE FILDES, R.A., 1870.
FOR A BACKGROUND TO ONE OF "EDWIN DROOD" ILLUSTRATIONS, 'UP THE RIVER.' (*p. xxvii.*)

LUKE FILDES, R.A.,

AS AN ILLUSTRATOR.

WHEN instinct first took the young Fildes to think of Art, the position of an illustrator seemed to him to mark the goal of his existence. To be an illustrator seemed, in fact, one of the glorious privileges of life — a position from which he could survey the world, if he could only acquire skill enough by which he could play upon the sentiment of the human race.

In the comparatively few years he spent as an illustrator of books his dream was more than realised, and he lived to know that his illustrations were a real power in the land. What if since then he has discovered that his dream, even when realised, was only the stepping-stone to greater achievements? None the less was his youthful ambition healthy, and the training it gave was of the greatest possible use in fitting him for what, later, he found was his real life's work.

After his studies at the National Art-Training School, where, it will be remembered, he won two scholarships in yearly succession, he was ready to try his 'prentice hand on original drawings. These were the days— about 1865 — before photography had come to be employed for transferring the drawings to the wood block.

Even in 1880, when I first joined the staff of THE ART JOURNAL, photography was only beginning to be used for the more complicated blocks, and the majority were drawn on the wood. In 1865, therefore, there was a good demand for illustrators to draw on the block, and it was to this that Fildes gave his attention.

His first illustrations were for a publication by Cassell's of "Foxe's Book of Martyrs," but the designer now says they ought to be buried in oblivion. After this, he made some drawings for *London Society*, and for many publications, among them the *Illustrated London News*, *Once a Week*, and *Good Words*. As related in the chapter, "Early Experiences," Fildes was soon working regularly for that most genial and generous of employers, Mr. W. L. Thomas. The relation then begun has ripened into life-long friendship, until now Mr. Fildes occupies a seat on the directing board of the *Graphic*, alongside his former chief.

THE UNWILLING SITTER. FROM THE "GRAPHIC." BY LUKE FILDES, R.A. (*p. xxviii.*)

H

Mr. Fildes' experiences as an illustrator are greatly bound up with the *Graphic*. When, in 1869, Mr. Thomas was arranging to start this paper, he asked his young friend to draw a striking picture, "To do them something good" was the actual expression. To use our artist's own words: "I was a young fellow then, trying to push my way, so I naturally felt greatly elated with the compliment. I said I would do what I could, and sent them the drawing to which they gave the place of honour in the first number of the *Graphic*. It was a picture of a number of casuals applying for tickets for the ward at the police-station. When I received the commission, I remember going to my lodgings, tumbling into an easy-chair, and wondering what I should do. I thought and smoked, walked about the room, when suddenly I remembered being much struck by the terrible pathos of a sight which I had seen in my nightly wanderings in the streets, some years ago when I first came to London, and I there and then made the sketch."

This subject was the 'Applicants for Admission to a Casual Ward,' and of the first idea, the design as set down on paper to see how it came, we give a reproduction at page

and ultimate friendship of Charles Dickens, and this is one of the most precious memories of a life spent amongst notabilities. Dickens had made the preliminary arrangements for his tragic "Edwin Drood," but there was a difficulty about who should be the illustrator, and he consulted Mr. Millais and Mr. W. P. Frith. These artists, too, were at a loss to lay their finger on the right illustrator, when luckily the first number of the *Graphic* appeared. Immediately Mr. Millais and Mr. Frith said, "This is the man for Dickens," and the paper was sent to the novelist.

Dickens had always been successful with his chief illustrator, H. K. Browne, "Phiz," and it is the fact that this artist's plates very often greatly helped the success of the books. But

ORIGINAL SKETCHES FOR "EDWIN DROOD" ILLUSTRATION, ENTITLED 'JASPER'S SACRIFICE.'
MISS ROSA BUD.   (*p. xxvii.*)

MR. JOHN JASPER.   (*p. xxvii.*)

two. The drawing was afterwards rendered on a larger wood-block, and appeared in the first number of the *Graphic*. The further development of this subject is told earlier in these pages, when treating of the large oil painting which became the sensation of the Royal Academy of 1874.

It is curious to observe how intimately this picture of 'The Casuals' is bound up with Mr. Fildes' career. In the first place it gained him the valuable favour of the *Graphic*; afterwards it was the picture which gave him his chance of being an Associate of the Royal Academy, for although he was not elected until 1879, 'The Casuals' had marked him as a certain Associate when vacancy permitted.

Moreover, 'The Casuals' gained Fildes the approbation

"Phiz" had been struck with severe paralysis in 1867, and although recovered from this attack and able to do some work, he was not equal to illustrate the volume then in preparation.[*] "Phiz" had been succeeded by Mr. Marcus Stone, who illustrated "Our Mutual Friend." But for "The Mystery of Edwin Drood," Dickens again sought a change, and he welcomed the newcomer. However, he was businesslike and cautious, and asked to see specimens of Fildes' other work, especially some drawings of ladies for his heroine. When he had seen the specimens, Dickens wrote to him in January, 1870 (only six months before his death), "I beg to thank you for the highly meritorious and interesting specimens of your art that you have had the kindness to send me. I return them herewith, having examined them with the greatest pleasure. . . . I can honestly assure you that I entertain the greatest admiration for your remarkable powers."

Fildes took extraordinary pains to follow the story of Edwin Drood from month to month, and he was so shrewd in his guesses towards the mystery that Dickens became

ORIGINAL SKETCH FOR THE EMPTY CHAIR. (*p. xxviii.*)

afraid he would be unable to keep the public from guessing too soon the point he was so carefully concealing. Yet Fildes really knew very little more than a careful reader of the book could divine, and the mystery—which was probably the mystery of the way the discovery of the murder came about— remains as much a mystery as ever. To quote our artist's own words: "He did, at my solicitation, occasionally tell me something—at first charily—for he said it was essential

to this reserve, which also excluded his family, it is curious to note that Charles Collins, his son-in-law, and brother of Wilkie Collins, who designed the wrapper with the enigmatical scenes conveying an idea of the general story, had not the faintest notion what they meant. He did them under Dickens' directions, but was told nothing of the story. Collins was to have been the illustrator, but health interfered, and Fildes came on the scene.

Reproductions of several of the "Edwin Drood" drawings are here printed, and from these it will be seen that Fildes, as an artist of character without caricature, attained a higher level than any of Dickens' illustrators have reached. 'Durdles cautions Mr. Sapsea against boasting' is probably the best of all, and although the original sketch we reproduce is a little confused, with the aid of the illustrations in Dickens' book all the characters can be found. Besides Durdles and Sapsea, there are in the drawing Jasper, the Dean, and Tope. Another drawing, p. 26, is a study for the design called 'Jasper's Sacrifice,' wherein the yet undiscovered murderer

THE EMPTY CHAIR, GAD'S HILL—NINTH OF JUNE, 1870. THE WOOD ENGRAVING ISSUED BY THE "GRAPHIC." (*p. xxviii.*)

to carefully preserve the "mystery" from general knowledge to sustain the interest of the book, and later, he appeared to have complete confidence in my discretion." In reference

reveals his love to Rosa, the fiancée of Edwin Drood, the one who has so mysteriously disappeared.

"Dickens, during the time I knew him—from December,

1869, to June, 1870—lived opposite the Marble Arch, where I often saw him, and, on his return to Gad's Hill, he invited me to stay with him there to go over the ground together to visit the scenes where the story was laid. I remember well the twenty-fourth and last was decided on, and we were to visit

"A LITTLE BLUE-FLANNEL BUNDLE WAS BROUGHT IN FOR INSPECTION," IN THE "CORNHILL MAGAZINE," JUNE, 1873. BY LUKE FILDES, R.A.   (*p. xxviii.*)

the scene, where he told me he himself had not been since he was a child.   Only twelve drawings were made, and six of them after Dickens' death.   I was going down to Gad's Hill on the 10th of June, and my luggage was packed ready to go, when I read his death in the morning paper."

The sudden death of the novelist, on June 9th, 1870, changed everything. All the same, "at the request of the family, who wished me to fulfil the desire of the great writer, they asked me after the funeral to come and stay with them, and it was then, while in the house of mourning, I conceived the idea of ' The Empty Chair,' and at once got my colours from London, and, with their permission, made the water-colour drawing a very faithful record of his library; and stayed with them until they left the house prior to the sale."

This was the close of Mr. Fildes' continuous work as an Illustrator, for it occurred at the moment when he felt a painter in oils was his true vocation, and he has done very little black-and-white work since then.

The ' Unwilling Sitter,' being the first efforts of the London police in photography, was a supplement to the *Graphic,* and ' A little Blue-flannel Bundle ' was an illustration prepared for a story —" Willows," a sketch in the *Cornhill Magazine* of 1873. The 'Found Dead' appeared in *The World* Christmas number in 1878. Fildes also made a series of illustrations to works by Charles Lever and W. M. Thackeray.

It will be observed that the earlier drawings on blocks are signed " S. L. Fildes," the artist having been christened Samuel Luke Fildes. But when he began painting he was advised to drop the initials, and employ only his home name of " Luke" Fildes. He had never been called Samuel, and therefore there was no change, except in the signature on his works. Every painting, even from the earliest, appears to have been signed "Luke Fildes," but the drawings have usually "S. L. Fildes."

Coming from an old Puritanic stock, whose children were mostly named after some saint of the Old or New Testament, this child, being born on October 18, was named Luke, because it was that saint's day. Little did the father and mother think that their resolve was prophetic, for St. Luke is the patron saint of artists, and it was appropriate that the future painter should be so christened. Luke, nevertheless, is a name rather uncommon amongst artists. There was, however, a Luke Clennell, a pupil of Thomas Bewick, who painted exquisitely in water-colour.

Luke Fildes is both easily pronounced and readily remembered. It may be pointed out that the name is spoken in one syllable only. It was originally written Fyldes, having a sound that would rhyme with the banker's name, Childs—a matter of little real importance except that occasionally people hesitate over it and sometimes render it in two syllables.

DURDLES CAUTIONS MR. SAPSEA AGAINST BOASTING.
SKETCH FOR ILLUSTRATION OF "EDWIN DROOD." BY LUKE FILDES, R.A. (*p. xxvii.*)

THE HOUSE AND STUDIO OF LUKE FILDES, R.A.

LUKE FILDES, R.A.

THE MAN AND THE STUDIO.

IT is no part of an artistic monograph on a living painter to give too minute details of the private life of the artist under consideration. Yet there are certain surroundings of a studio which, being set forth without intruding into his home and hearth, help to a better understanding of the artist and of his productions.

Not that it is necessarily a spacious residence which bids an artist reach his highest flight. Turner's later life, to take one instance alone, proves the reverse. But an artist usually surrounds himself with what he most likes and admires, and we naturally expect his environment to have its proper influence on his work.

Mr. Fildes lives in the most desirable part of Holland Park, in Melbury Road, whose every other resident is a member of the Royal Academy. The President's studio is only over the roadway, and within a couple of minutes' walk of Mr. Fildes' house. Should Mr. Fildes seek a little fresh air before calling to see his revered chief, in one direction he would pass the studios of Mr. Marcus Stone, R.A., of Mr. G. F. Watts, R.A., and of Mr. Val Prinsep, R.A.; and in the other direction he would pass the door of Mr. Colin Hunter, A.R.A., the painter of Scottish landscapes and fishermen.

Overlooking the famous Holland House and Park from one point of view, from another he looks out on Kensington High Road, after allowing his eye to rest on the road leading to his own gate. A good-sized red-brick house, looking, like its owner, cheerful in its aspect and dignified in its tone.

The studio is, of course, upstairs—not very far, however, only one flight. Here, in a salon which might be called a hall, Mr. Fildes receives his known artistic visitors, and sometimes also paints the portraits to which so much of his life has been recently given up. Farther on, the studio opens into another salon, entirely open by glass windows to the east and north, ceiling and walls in these directions being all of glass. In this latter most of his work is, at the least, completed. There he finds fault, if he can, with the work which may have appeared finished in the studio proper. There he takes final farewell of the canvas which may, perhaps, have cost him several months' work.

In the larger studio Mr. Fildes painted 'The Doctor.' Inside his lofty ceilinged *atelier* he erected the cottage interior, and from that and his many previous experiences he made the picture of 'The Doctor,' at first without models, and only at the last from life. It may be noted in

LUKE FILDES, R.A.

1

passing that the Doctor has considerable personal likeness to the artist himself. At page 12 our illustration, done by Mr. Cleaver originally for the *Daily Graphic*, shows the artist at work with the cottage interior inside his studio.

Surrounding the studio are examples of the chief reproductions, Goupil photogravures or mezzotints, made from his pictures. Here and there is a sketch from a brother painter, an elegant escritoire, with book - case and lounges and fireplace—all as cosy in winter as in summer it is free and open.

The garden, adjoining the grounds of the historic Holland House, covers about half an acre, and in certain parts farthest from the house little or nothing of human

THE GARDEN DOOR.

children are about. Our country cousins and foreign friends never thoroughly understand the beauty and isolation of many houses in London, well within the four-mile cab circle from Charing Cross. It is the stranger's conceit that London contains nothing but houses, that gardens are unknown, and even green trees have little or no existence. Let them think of Mr. Fildes' beautiful surroundings, and bear in mind that practically there exists no important street in London where trees or gardens are not visible from some part of it.

I remember calling at the studio one day, about two years ago, and finding Mr. Fildes much agitated. Just before he had had an alarm

habitations can be seen, and only the birds singing disturb the quietness on a summer afternoon, unless Mr. Fildes' of fire; something more than an alarm, in fact, for in a few minutes flames and smoke appeared in a way to appal

THE STUDIO OF LUKE FILDES, R.A.

the heart of the stoutest. The painter had just finished the portrait of the Princess of Wales, and the canvas was standing in the large studio. The weather was cold (it was November, 1893), and a good stove fire was necessary to heat the rooms. Unluckily, a living cinder fell from the stove, and it rolled on to the corner of a curtain where the inner studio divides from the other. In one moment almost, the drapery took fire, and flames leaped up the curtain.

THE ENTRANCE TO THE HOUSE.

Mr. Fildes was at lunch below, but happily a servant observed the approaching disaster. In an instant the artist was upstairs, and his first action was to seize the portrait of the Princess and take it to a safer place. Then, accompanied by his gardener, he combated the gradually increasing fire. Again and again he seemed about to be driven back; even the gardener trembled at the appearance of things, and at one moment tried to pull the artist down from the ladder he had set up, beating the flames, and pouring the water the frightened domestics brought to him.

Within ten minutes the fire was subdued, and all danger over; but meanwhile the neighbourhood was alarmed, and policemen and firemen hurried to help. Two fire-engines and a multitude of hose-pipes put in their appearance; but all they had to do was to pour more water on the burning curtains, which Mr. Fildes had been able to throw out of the studio window into the garden.

I dwell in this detail on what turned out to be but a trifling material loss because it shows the character of Mr. Fildes, the pertinacity and fearlessness of the man, who fought, single-handed and successfully, to extinguish the fire. His is no character to look on and let others work; when danger or difficulty approaches him he does not shrink from duty, but gamely goes for the enemy, and even when others deem the task too heavy, he manfully sticks to the post and comes out the victor—he is, in fact, a manly man, and, at the same time, a genial friend and a generous opponent.

DAVID CROAL THOMSON.

THE GARDEN FRONT, SHOWING STUDIOS ABOVE.

LIST OF PICTURES

EXHIBITED AT THE ROYAL ACADEMY; BEING THE PRINCIPAL WORKS OF LUKE FILDES, R.A.

1872.—' Fair Quiet and Sweet Rest.' (Illustrated page 1.)
1873.—' Simpletons ' ('The Sweet River.' Line engraving.)
1874.—' Applicants for Admission to a Casual Ward.' (Illustrated page 5.)
1875.—' Betty.' (Illustrated page 23.)
1876.—' The Widower.' (Illustrated page 4.)
1877.—' Playmates.'
1879.—' Return of the Penitent.' (Illustrated page 7.)
1881.—' Doubts.'
    ' Dolly.'
    ' A Venetian.'
1882.—' Nina.'
1883.—' The Village Wedding.' (Illustrated page 11.)
1884.—' Venetian Life.'
    ' A Venetian Flower-Girl.' (Illustrated page 18.)
1885.—' Venetians.'
    ' Rosetta.'
1887.—' Mrs. Luke Fildes.' (Illustrated page 19.)
    ' Mrs. W. L. Agnew.'
1888.—' A Schoolgirl.' (' Phyllis.' Illustrated page 8.)
1889.—' An Al-Fresco Toilette.' (Photogravure plate.)
    ' Sisters.' (Illustrated page 20.)

1890.—' A Daughter of the Ghetto.'
    ' Mrs. Thomas Agnew.'
    ' Mrs. Robert Borwick.'
    ' Portrait of a Lady '
1891.—' Mrs. Lockett Agnew.'
    ' The Doctor.' (Etching.)
1892.—' Mrs. Edwin Tate.'
    ' Ethel,' daughter of T. H. Ismay, Esq
    ' Mrs. Herbert S. Leon.'
    ' Jas. J. Bibby, Esq.'
    ' Mrs. Bibby.' (Illustrated page 20.)
1893.—' Portrait of a Lady.' (Illustrated page 20.)
    ' Mrs. Elliot Lees.'
    ' G. B. Wieland, Esq.'
1894.—' Mrs. Robert Yerburgh.'
    ' H.R.H. The Princess of Wales.' (Illustrated page 21.)
    ' Mrs. Pantia Ralli.'
1895.—' Mrs. Johnson-Ferguson.'
    ' Mrs. Arthur James.'
    ' Robert Yerburgh, Esq., M.P.'
    ' Frank Bibby, Esq.'

IN CHESTER—EARLY PENCIL SKETCH BY LUKE FILDES, R.A.

Lightning Source UK Ltd.
Milton Keynes UK
UKHW022004141222
413947UK00005B/78